BARRY'S MATHEMAGICAL JOURNEY

Place Value
Volume 1: Book 2

WRITTEN BY BARRY R. BECK JR.
ILLUSTRATED BY MANDY B. JOHNSON

Written By: Barry R. Beck Jr.
Illustrated By: Mandy B. Johnson
Edited By: Nalani Butler

© 2025 Barry R. Beck Jr.

ISBN 9781967082421 (Hardcover)
ISBN 9781967082438 (Paperback)
ISBN 9781967082445 (eBook)
Library of Congress Control Number - 2025913705

All rights reserved. This book or any portion thereof may not be reproduced in any form without permission from the copyright holder, except as permitted by U.S. Copyright Law.

Printed in the United States of America

BookButler Publishing Company
Upper Marlboro, MD 20774

TheBookButler.com

BookButler Publishing Company titles may be purchased in bulk for educational, business, fundraising, or sales promotional use. For information, please email: info@thebookbutler.com

This Book is Dedicated To...
My Mother

...The real MVP.

Now that we have ten unifix cubes, let's connect the ten units to create one group of ten. This will help us count more easily.

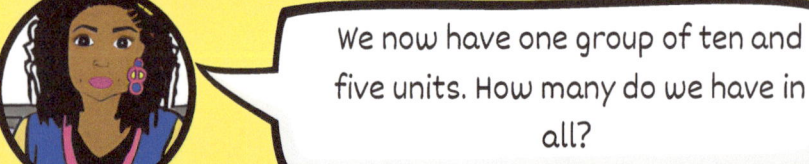

We now have one group of ten and five units. How many do we have in all?

 We have fifteen, Ms. Hall. We have one group of ten and five unifix cubes left over.

 That is correct Jorge. Barry, do you understand that the number fifteen has one group of ten and five ones?

 Yes! So my homework is correct, Ms. Hall. I just didn't know why it was correct.

 Yes, Barry! Now Jorge, how can we fix your homework to make it correct? Think about what we just did with the unifix cubes.

 I have fifteen circles. I can circle ten of the circles to make one group of ten. Then I will have five circles left over. I have one group of ten and five ones.

"Buenos dias, Jorge and Barry"

"Are both of you ready to show me how you did your homework last night?"

"Buenos dias, Ms. Hall. Yes!"

HOMEWORK

How many tens and ones are needed to make the number 53?

Yes, Barry, both of you were able to answer the question correctly! Both of you used different objects to answer the question, but the strategy was the same. It doesn't matter what type of object is being used. What matters is you put the items in groups of ten and had ones left over. That's place value!

I am so proud of both of you! Tomorrow I will not be with you. Both of you will be back with everyone else.

Ms. Hall, what if we don't understand when we're back in class? Second grade math is finally starting to make sense.

You both will be fine. Just remember what we did over the past two days. Do not forget the strategy that I have shown you.

Okay!

Hey, Barry, are you okay?

No! Mrs. Moon just kicked me out of class because I asked a question!

Really? There has to be more to it than that, Barry.

No, she hates me!

Mrs. Moon does not hate you, Barry.

Jorge, you're right.

I thought about what Ms. Hall had us do for homework the other day. We didn't have unifix cubes. We had to use something else to help solve the problem.

Hey, boys, are y'all ready for some math?

 Ms. Hall, I had trouble understanding a question Mrs. Moon gave the class yesterday. She wouldn't let me use unifix cubes.

 Barry, when you saw the problem did you think of a way to solve it without using unifix cubes?

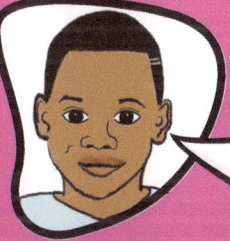 No, I thought since we were in school we had to use them.

 The other day, while doing your homework, what did you use to solve the problem?

 I used the candy my father brought home.

 Correct! There are always other ways to help solve problems. You just have to use your imagination.

 Imagination? To help solve math problems?

 Yes, there are things everywhere that can help you. Just be creative.

 I guess, Ms. Hall. Since we can't use unifix cubes, can I draw something that will help me solve the problem?

 Yes, that's what I did!

 Ms. Hall, does it matter what we draw to answer the question?

 No, Barry, you can use whatever you like.

 Okay, I am going to use dots to help me solve the problem.

Barry says excitedly, Mom, I did it. I finally did it!
What did you do, Barry?
I understand second grade math!

That's great, Barry! I'm about to go to the grocery store. Do you want to go with me?
Ugh, okay.

 Yes, Barry! How was school?

 School was great! I finally answered one of Mrs. Moon's questions right.

 That's great!

 Mom, is it okay if I go over to Jorge's house tomorrow after school? We have a test in two days, and we want to study together.

 Let me reach out to Jorge's mom to make sure it is okay!

 Thanks, Mom.

Barry and Jorge begin putting the leaves in groups of ten with the leftover leaves that cannot be grouped in tens, they make ones.

"Barry, while putting the leaves in groups of ten, make rods like Mrs. Hall showed us."

"Great idea, Jorge, that way they're easier to count."

> After creating rods with the leaves and counting them, Barry and Jorge notice that there are 57 leaves.

 You will be fine, son. You've been working really hard and it will pay off.

 Okay, mom! Mom? Where's Abuela? I want Barry to meet her.

 Barry looking confused: Huh, Jorge? What is an Abuela?

 Jorge says with a smile on his face: Barry, that's my grandma.

 Oh, okay. I call my grandma Big Ma.

 Yes, Barry, that's Jorge's grandma. Coming from different backgrounds, we refer to our elders differently. But it all means the same thing.

Characters and Relationships

- How would you describe Barry and Jorge's friendship by the end of the story? How did it grow?
- What role did Ms. Hall play in helping Barry and Jorge build confidence in math?
- How did Barry's and Jorge's families support them in their learning?
- In what ways did Barry and Jorge help each other understand math?

Challenges and Emotions

- How did Barry feel when Mrs. Moon didn't allow him to use unifix cubes? Why?
- Why was Jorge nervous before the math test? How did he overcome it?
- What were some emotional changes Barry and Jorge experienced throughout the story?
- How did Mr. Smith help Barry manage his emotions after getting upset in class?

School Experiences

- What teaching strategies did Ms. Hall use to help Barry and Jorge understand place value?
- Why did Barry struggle at first with math even though he had the correct answer?
- How did Mrs. Moon's expectations challenge Barry in the classroom?
- How did homework assignments help Barry and Jorge become more confident in school?

BOOK TALK

Learning and Growth

- What did Barry and Jorge learn about solving place value problems without unifix cubes?
- How did drawing dots help Barry understand tens and ones?
- Why was it important for Barry and Jorge to use everyday objects like beans and candy?
- What evidence shows that Barry and Jorge grew academically and emotionally during the story?

Cultural Understanding

- What did Barry learn about Jorge's culture during their friendship?
- How did Jorge's grandmother support his learning, even though she didn't speak English fluently?
- Why is it important to recognize and respect the different ways families communicate and support learning?
- How did food and language help Jorge connect with math in his home environment?

ABOUT THE AUTHOR

Barry, a dedicated math teacher residing in Henrico, VA, has spent years inspiring students with his passion for numbers. His passion for numbers began in Virginia, where he helped countless children build confidence and excitement in math through his engaging and creative teaching style.

Now, as an author, Barry is expanding his reach far beyond the walls of his own school. With his first book, he's connecting with students, families, and educators across school districts and even in other states. Barry is excited about what's next and remains committed to helping others see the magic, joy, and real-life value of math.

ABOUT THE ILLUSTRATOR

Mandy, an artist and educator residing in Alexandria, VA, brings her passion for visual arts and teaching together to create vibrant, engaging learning experiences. With a background in visual arts, she fills her classroom with creativity, using her artistic talents to help students connect with lessons in meaningful and memorable ways.

As the illustrator of Barry's Mathemagical Journey, Mandy has brought her lifelong dream to life, turning stories into vivid, magical worlds through her art. She's now exploring new ways to tap into her creativity, using illustration and design to inspire not just students, but people of all ages to discover the joy in learning, imagination, and self-expression.

KEEP UP WITH BARRY'S MATHEMAGICAL JOURNEY!

Barry's Mathemagical Journey Vol. 1

Barry's Mathemagical Journey Interactive Workbook

Follow -US-

📷 @mathemagical_journey

 www.mathemagicaljourney.com